THE CLOCK

TURNING POINT INVENTIONS

THE CLOCK

TRENT DUFFY

Foldout illustration by Toby Welles

Atheneum Books for Young Readers

NEW YORK   LONDON   TORONTO   SYDNEY   SINGAPORE

Atheneum Books for Young Readers
An imprint of Simon & Schuster
Children's Publishing Division
1230 Avenue of the Americas
New York, New York 10020

FIRST EDITION

Produced by
CommonPlace Publishing
2 Morse Court
New Canaan, Connecticut 06840

Art Director: Samuel N. Antupit
Editor: Sharon AvRutick
Picture Research: Jean Martin
Production Design: Cheung/Crowell Design

Printed in Hong Kong through Global Interprint

10 9 8 7 6 5 4 3 2 1

ISBN 0-689-82814-4

Library of Congress
Card Catalog Number: 99-65242

For my mother

Endpapers
This plate from a mid-nineteenth-century French treatise on horology by Claudius Saunier
shows part of the mechanism of a typical pocket watch of that period.

Page 1
John Harrison holds his prize-winning invention, H-4, in this portrait by painter Thomas King.

Pages 2–3
Unlike most wristwatches, this unusual model does not have a dial. Its hour and minute hands
are connected directly to the mechanism.

CONTENTS

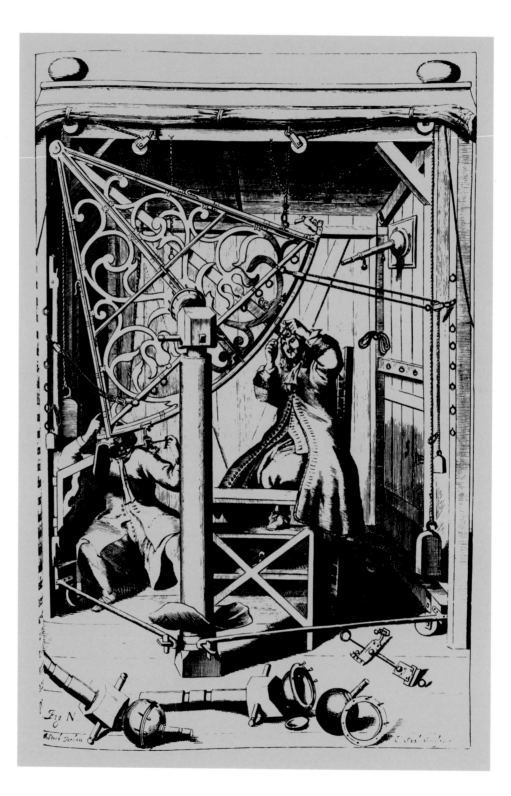

1

THE BEGINNINGS OF TIME

What time did you get up today? How often have you looked at your watch in the last few hours? Do you know how to set the time on your VCR to tape a show? When Daylight Saving Time begins or ends, do you help reset all the clocks at home?

So many of your activities are guided by the time. An alarm clock rings or a clock radio turns on your favorite station in order to wake you up in the morning. Your gym teacher uses a precision stopwatch to determine how quickly you run the 100-yard dash. You program the microwave to heat a snack. Like everyone else, you rely on many timekeeping devices each day — so many, in fact, that it's difficult to imagine a world with no clocks, no precise schedules, and a completely different sense of time.

The first humans, however, had little need to know the exact time. They got all the information they needed about the passage of time from observing the alternation of day and night and the rhythm of the seasons. They would sleep at night, and hunt and gather in the daytime. They surely noticed that their hunting and gathering was more successful in the warm weather months than in the cold.

Opposite
An astronomer and his assistant prepare to make observations of the nighttime sky in this seventeenth-century German print. Such observations have long been used for keeping track of the flow of time.

Then, after thousands of years, people began to establish the first permanent societies in the fertile river valleys of China, India, and the Middle East. Early astronomers began to pay attention to the sky. Their observations showed that the movement of the sun, moon, and stars all followed patterns: The sun rose each morning in the eastern sky and set each evening in the west. There was a new moon (the phase of the moon when it seems dark) every twenty-nine or thirty days. After twelve new moons, the seasons were roughly back to where they had been. A year had passed.

The ancient Babylonians, who lived in what is now Iraq, were among the first people to develop an actual calendar, a system of naming and keeping track of the days. Based on astronomers' observations of the regularly occurring new moon, their calendar included twelve months and 360 days. The Babylonians also divided each day into twelve hours of daytime and twelve hours of night.

This calendar worked quite well. In fact, such lunar calendars are still used in the Jewish and Muslim religions. But since the earth takes more than 360 days (about 365¼ days, to be precise) to complete a revolution around the sun, after several decades, the difference of 5¼ days every year began to add up, and the Babylonian lunar calendar no longer corresponded to the progression of the yearly seasons.

The Egyptians, whose highly developed early civilization arose in the fertile Nile Valley, developed a calendar of their own, and it was the first to have 365 days to the year. No one knows for sure when this first solar calendar was developed, but archaeologists have determined that it was in use by 4241 B.C.

Other societies made efforts of their own to keep track of time. The Mayans, the Hindus, the Chinese, the Japanese, and other peoples developed their own calendars as well.

Sometime between 1900 B.C. and 1600 B.C., Neolithic peoples in southern England constructed a ring made up of enormous stones. Today we think that this circle, known as Stonehenge, was used on religious or ceremonial occasions.

The Aztecs, the most powerful civilization in Mexico in the fifteenth century, learned much from the civilizations that preceded them. Their calendar stone shows the sun god in the middle; surrounding him are symbols of earth, air, water, and fire. The next ring has twenty divisions, corresponding to the days of the Aztec month.

There were eighteen months of twenty days each, as well as five extra days, for a total of 365 days.

What we know for sure is that it was also one of the world's first timekeepers, in the sense that it is keyed to the summer solstice, the longest day of the year. If you are standing in the middle of the circle that day, you will see the sun rising exactly over the top of one of the outer stones.

As calendars developed to keep track of the flow of the years, the cues the sun provides about the time of day — dawn, sunrise, noon (when the sun reaches its highest point in the sky), sunset, and darkness — were no longer enough. Someone somewhere, perhaps in Babylonia or Egypt, stuck a stick or a stone into the earth and noticed the movement of the shadow it cast as the sun traveled from east to west. People began to mark the area the shadow

Tall towers called
obelisks dotted the
Egyptian landscape.
Those that stood in
public plazas served
as sundials.

would cross with lines indicating the hours. They made sundials to use these shadows to determine the approximate time.

Beginning around 1500 B.C., the ancient Egyptians made massive sundials. They built obelisks (stone towers as much as eighty feet tall) in the middle of plazas. A semicircle was then marked around the northern half of the base of the obelisk, divided by twelve lines to indicate the hours. Centuries later, the Greeks and Romans were still using this method of timekeeping; in fact, the Romans even used some actual Egyptian sundials. They removed at least twenty obelisks from Egypt and set them up in public plazas in their own city. Some of these obelisks, which are now more than three thousand years old, are still standing today.

The Romans made smaller sundials as well. One kind, the hemistyle, used a rod or tiny obelisk (called a style) sitting in the center of a bowl on a column about two or three feet high. You might say that the tinier portable models, only one and a half inches across, were the ancient equivalent of the pocket watch.

As the size of sundials decreased, their accuracy and usefulness improved. Since the length and angle of a shadow changes depending on the season, the

Left
The bowls of sundials were often inscribed with a series of semicircles. Three semicircles are clearly visible in this Roman model; the intersecting vertical lines show the hours as the shadow cast by the rod, or style, moves across them.

Right
In Europe, sundials took on many stylized forms.

Romans marked the bowl of a sundial or the plaza around an obelisk with a series of circles, each divided with lines indicating the twelve hours of daylight. The outermost circle showed the hours at the shortest day of the year, and the innermost corresponded to the hours at midsummer. This improvement allowed the Romans to tell time rather accurately all year long.

Even as sundials were refined, though, their disadvantages were very obvious: They were no good on cloudy days and couldn't work at all at night. Other inventions were developed to get around these problems, but unlike sundials, these devices couldn't be used to tell time. They could only indicate that a certain amount of time had elapsed.

Starting around 2800 B.C., Egyptians developed the water clock in order to keep track of the hours of the night. The inside of a water clock's container, usually a stone bowl, was inscribed with marks. Water would drip steadily into (or out of) the container, and people were able to tell how much time had passed by using the marks to compare the water level at a given moment with a previous level. Later, in Greece and Rome, water clocks were used to limit the duration of a speech in court or in the Roman senate.

Making accurate water clocks was difficult. Not only did the flow of water

Left
Even as clockmaking advanced, people still consulted sundials. This model, which is combined with a compass, dates from eighteenth-century France.

Right
Made in China, this portable sundial would be most accurate from March to September within the latitudes of that country. Fully portable, it could be folded up to slip into a pocket.

have to be carefully controlled, but the bowl had to be shaped very precisely. In addition, the water would gradually rub tiny bits of stone away from the opening it constantly passed through, thus increasing its size. As the hole gradually grew bigger, the water would flow out more quickly, and the time it took the container to fill or empty would no longer correspond to what the scale of marks inscribed on the basin indicated. By 1400 B.C., Egyptian clockmakers learned to line the hole with a hard metal, which was more resistant than stone to erosion.

The sandglass is similar to the water clock. It was developed in Europe later, after glassmaking was more advanced — probably around A.D. 1300. Two glass bulbs containing sand, finely ground eggshells, or powdered porcelain were joined at their necks, and the contents of the top bulb would run slowly through the narrow necks into the bottom bulb. This took a set amount of time. (An hourglass is a sandglass in which the process takes exactly an hour.) When the top glass was empty, the sandglass could be turned upside down to begin

the process again. Sandglasses were particularly useful in the winter, when the water in water clocks might freeze.

During the so-called Dark Ages, after the fall of Rome in the year A.D. 476, Roman Catholic monks in western Europe developed their own system of time-keeping so that they would chant certain prayers at specific times of day. These times were called canonical hours. The monks used water clocks, but they would also keep track of the hours with candle clocks, which historians believe were invented in England in the ninth century. Candle clocks were simply candles made to a precise height and width, so that they would take a set amount of time (typically, four or eight hours) to burn. The candles also had marks for individual hours etched into their sides, so that they could serve to tell time (as long as you knew the hour at which they'd been lit) as well as mark the passage of hours.

Water clocks and other innovations were not limited to Europe. The Arabs were building elaborate examples in A.D. 800. It was in China, however, that the most elaborate and accurate water clocks were built, especially between the seventh and fourteenth centuries.

Left
With this modern reproduction of a candle clock, one can judge the passage of a certain amount of time.

Center and right
Oil lamps were also used as clocks. In both of these lamps, the lines on the chamber in which the oil is stored can be consulted to determine how much time has elapsed since the chamber was full.

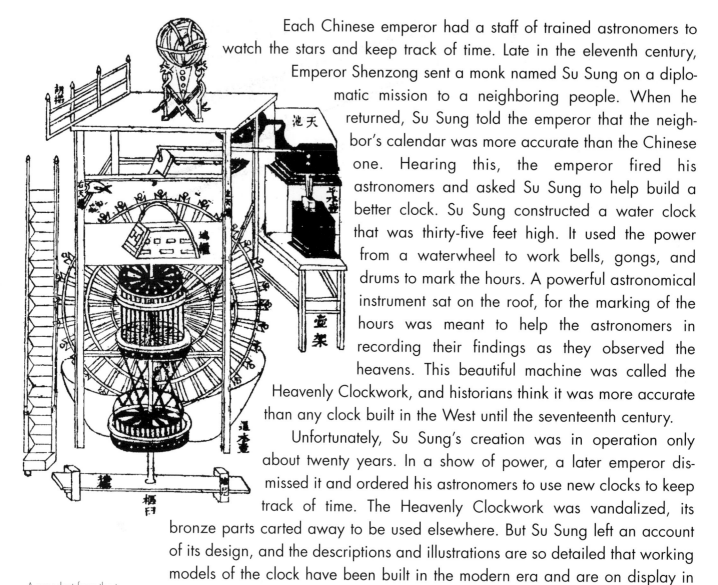

Each Chinese emperor had a staff of trained astronomers to watch the stars and keep track of time. Late in the eleventh century, Emperor Shenzong sent a monk named Su Sung on a diplomatic mission to a neighboring people. When he returned, Su Sung told the emperor that the neighbor's calendar was more accurate than the Chinese one. Hearing this, the emperor fired his astronomers and asked Su Sung to help build a better clock. Su Sung constructed a water clock that was thirty-five feet high. It used the power from a waterwheel to work bells, gongs, and drums to mark the hours. A powerful astronomical instrument sat on the roof, for the marking of the hours was meant to help the astronomers in recording their findings as they observed the heavens. This beautiful machine was called the Heavenly Clockwork, and historians think it was more accurate than any clock built in the West until the seventeenth century.

Unfortunately, Su Sung's creation was in operation only about twenty years. In a show of power, a later emperor dismissed it and ordered his astronomers to use new clocks to keep track of time. The Heavenly Clockwork was vandalized, its bronze parts carted away to be used elsewhere. But Su Sung left an account of its design, and the descriptions and illustrations are so detailed that working models of the clock have been built in the modern era and are on display in European museums.

Although the Chinese were more technologically advanced clockmakers than Westerners at the time, they never followed up on Su Sung's Heavenly Clockwork by trying to build more accurate timekeepers. Instead, the next major development in telling time would come from the West.

A woodcut from the turn of the twelfth century shows the inner workings of Su Sung's Heavenly Clockwork. Astronomers used the device on the roof, called an armillary sphere, to study the stars in the night sky.

In this modern-day model of the Heavenly Clockwork, the water-wheel and gears can be seen on the enormous water clock's first two levels.

2

THE INVENTION OF THE MECHANICAL CLOCK

The nobility and clergy of medieval Europe wanted to be remembered for their good deeds and accomplishments. So kings and dukes, popes and bishops, and even wealthy knights hired chroniclers to record their lives. The documents chroniclers left behind reveal many details about life in the West especially after the year 1000, and one thing they reveal for sure is that medieval people had a very different attitude about numbers than we do today. Even though chronicles were mostly accurate, the numbers in them were often so large that they defied belief. What mattered was that a figure helped present a vivid picture of what happened. The number of men killed in a battle, the height of a mountain pass, or the time it took to make a pilgrimage — all these could be exaggerated to make the chronicler's boss and his allies appear braver, stronger, or more devout.

The timekeeping devices in use in the early Middle Ages were part and parcel of this indifference to precise counting. Water clocks, which were the most widely used instrument, measured the flow of time, but they could not tell the exact hour. For most people, the daytime was divided into twelve hours, but these hours had no fixed value as they do now (sixty minutes, or $1/24$ of a day); they varied with the season, longer in summer and shorter in winter. The

Opposite
Giovanni de' Dondi designed the world's first astronomical clock around 1364. One of the dials displayed the time in his hometown, Mantua, Italy, and others showed the motion of the sun, the moon, and all the known planets of the time. This reproduction was made from the plans for the original, which was lost hundreds of years ago.

seven canonical hours used in religious institutions indicated when certain prayers were to be said, but they had little relationship to the concept of an hour as we know it.

As the medieval era continued, several factors combined to encourage a greater interest in measuring things precisely: the increase in trade; the growth of cities; the emergence of stronger nations, with central governments enforcing laws and collecting taxes; and a renewed interest in learning, which included a newfound curiosity about the world in general and about science and mathematics in particular. By the thirteenth century, a growing number of people throughout Europe had more and more reason to count things. Time began to be thought of as a succession of distinct moments, something that could be measured and kept track of, rather than something that just flowed through your hands.

It was in this climate that the first mechanical clock appeared in western Europe. Unfortunately, historians can tell us very little about this technological advance, as important as it is. They know that a mechanical clock — a clock powered by moving parts — was probably built sometime between 1275 and 1300. But they don't know the name of the inventor or exactly when, where, or how he or she made the breakthrough.

The earliest mechanical clocks seem to have varied considerably in their design, but in general, they used a system of interconnected gears (such as the ones that had already been used in inventions like the waterwheel). These time-keepers were powered by a stone that was rigged up to fall very slowly; later, clockmakers fashioned weights designed especially for this task of providing the clock's energy. A rope attached to the weight at one end was wound around a toothed wheel called a capstan, which, as it turned, moved a series of gears and other contraptions that kept track of the time. This whole section of the clock is known as its movement.

As "modern" as they were, the clocks were not very accurate by today's standards. The very best ones would gain or lose fifteen minutes in each

Opposite
The striking mechanism of the turret clock at the cathedral in Wells, England, which was built about 1392. The clock is the second oldest in the country and the first to be constructed with a dial.

The jacks at the top of the church tower in Udine, Italy, alternate striking the bell. These bronze automatons made in 1850 replaced the fourteenth-century originals, which were made of wood.

twenty-four-hour period, but most clocks gained or lost an hour a day. The highly developed sundials of the era actually told the time better than the vast majority of mechanical clocks until the late seventeenth century.

The first mechanical clocks were large, usually two to eight feet wide. They had no faces or hands — all they did was tick to mark the time. Most were just a collection of gears, interconnected within an open metal frame. If you saw one today, you probably wouldn't even recognize that it was a clock.

When one of the internal parts, the counting wheel, showed that an hour had passed, the striking wheel would sound a bell — once at one o'clock, twice at two o'clock, and so on. Before long, clockmakers made little mechanical men, called automatons, or jacks, to sound the hours. These jacks would move along a short track each hour, striking the bell to denote the proper number of hours. (In fact, the word "clock" is derived from the sounding of these bells. It was adapted into the English language from the French *cloche* and the German *Glocke*, both of which mean bell.)

These first mechanical clocks required a tremendous amount of upkeep. The handmade parts fit together imperfectly, causing abrasion, friction, and, all too frequently, breakdowns. As well as performing constant repairs, a clockkeeper also had to correct the time, resetting it against a sundial at high noon each day.

These early mechanical clocks must have seemed wondrous to the people of the Middle Ages. They were built at bigger churches and monasteries throughout the fourteenth century, and it became a matter of pride for a prosperous town to have a working clock. By the fifteenth century, they had been

The clock on the Town Hall of Prague, in the Czech Republic, was built around 1410. The lower dial is a yearly calendar. The outer circles of the upper dial tell the time, while the inner one is an astronomical calendar. The doors on either side of the sculpture at the top open to reveal automatons that toll the hours.

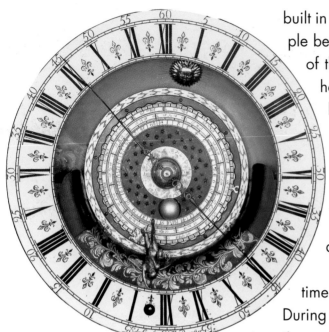

built in almost every large European town and city, and people began to think about time differently. Earlier, the length of the twelve daytime hours and twelve nighttime hours had varied with the season. But now that there were bells announcing every hour (more or less), things began to change. Time was becoming more of a solid concept, and its meaning — how long is an hour? — began to derive more from the accuracy of a machine (the mechanical clock) than from a natural phenomenon (the daily voyage of the sun across the sky).

Another major change in how people related to time stemmed from a change made to the clock itself. During this period, as the day moved on, clocks chimed fourteen times at "fourteen o'clock," twenty times at "twenty o'clock," and so on. Clockmakers realized that if the bell didn't have to toll so many times to announce the hour, the device would need less power. Therefore, the habit arose of dividing the day into two sets of twelve hours. This was the start of our current system of telling time, in which we have an 11:00 A.M. in the morning and an 11:00 P.M. late at night. (The abbreviations stand for *ante meridiem* and *post meridiem*, Latin for "before noon" and "after noon.")

Increasingly, starting in the mid-fourteenth century, clocks were built with dials — a circular panel that was the public "face" of the clock. The numerals 1 through 12 — usually in Roman numerals (I through XII) — were painted on the outer edge of the dial, and a hand, or arrowlike pointer, was mounted on the center of the dial. Attached to a gear behind the face, the hand slowly revolved around the dial, pointing to each number in sequence. Bells continued to sound the hours, however, because many people were illiterate and could not read the numbers on the dial. Now that clocks had faces, they were able to transmit other kinds of information. Town clocks often had special hands

Ioan. Stradanus invent.

Ioan. Galle excud.

HOROLOGIA FERREA.

Rota æqua ferrea ætherisq̃ voluitur,   *Recludit æquè et hæc et illa tempora.*

controlled by separate gears that would display the phase of the moon as well as a yearly calendar.

The next breakthrough in the history of the clock was an improvement in its power source. Galileo Galilei, the inventor of the telescope, sketched a mechanical clock in the 1630s that was powered by a pendulum. Near the end of his life, he asked his son to build the clock, but the man never got around to it. Galileo's sketches were buried amid the pile of papers he left behind at his death in 1642.

Fifteen years later, a Dutch astronomer and physicist named Christiaan Huygens built the world's first pendulum clock, just as Galileo had envisioned it. For the next hundred years, pendulum clocks were built all over Europe as

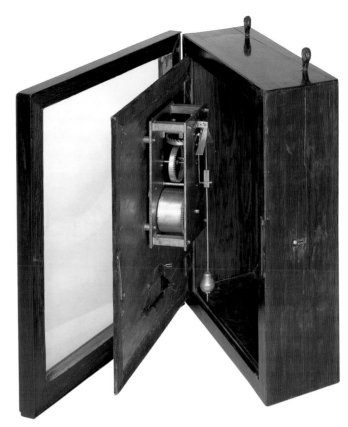

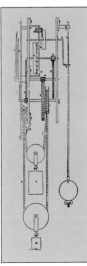

clockmakers tried to improve on Huygens's technological advance. English clockmakers developed a crucial part known as the anchor escapement. The escapement is the part of the clock that takes the energy from the power source, transmits it through the gears, and releases it in "beats" (often, one per second). The early mechanical clocks had primitive escapements that didn't regulate the beat very well. The new escapement, which resembled an anchor, fit on top of the first of the clock's toothed gears. Stimulated by the pendulum's motion, the anchor escapement rocked back and forth on this wheel, allowing it to advance one tooth and then blocking its further advance. When the pendulum returned, the escapement released another tooth. In this way, the anchor escapement controlled the rate at which the new pendulum clock beat, far

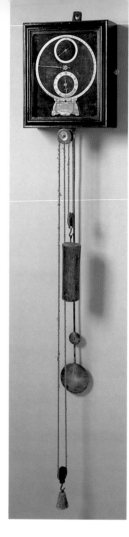

better and more consistently than had any of its ancestors.

Some models left the pendulum open to view. Others enclosed it in a protective long wooden box, which stood on a base. The movement and the dial sat on top. This latter kind of pendulum clock is called a longcase clock, but is more often known as a "grandfather" clock. Later, around 1730, Franz Anton Ketterer, a Swiss craftsman, put a wooden bird in a box over the dial. When it emerged each hour, it announced the time with the call of the cuckoo bird.

Pendulum clocks had one noticeable drawback: They had to remain motionless in order to keep accurate time. This was discovered when the clocks were taken on board ships or stagecoaches. The motion of the stagecoach interfered with the motion of the pendulum, causing the clock to run too fast or too slow.

The same thing happened on sea voyages, where changes in temperature and exposure to moisture made the clocks run even more poorly.

One other significant technological advance was the invention of the mainspring. Inventors discovered that energy was contained in a wound-up spring. As the spring unwound, the energy was released and could power a watch, a small portable clock. The earliest watches powered by a mainspring were so inaccurate that they were virtually useless, assuming you wanted to use them to tell the time. But they did serve another purpose: They were often carried in the pocket of a vest or other garment as a sign of social rank, meant to impress others.

Above
The earliest known surviving long pendulum clock was made by a Dutchman, Severyn Oosterwyck, in 1663.

Right
This Japanese table clock was spring driven.

Opposite
This English lantern clock, from about 1700, uses an anchor escapement (not visible in this side view).

3

JOHN HARRISON AND THE CHRONOMETRIC CLOCK

In the autumn of 1707, a fleet of five English warships headed home after defeating the French navy in a skirmish near Gibraltar, at the mouth of the Mediterranean Sea. Once they had rounded Spain, they sailed north across the Bay of Biscay, staying well away from the French coast. As they neared England, the fog closed in, so the navigators were unable to check their position. Admiral Sir Clowdisley Shovell thought he was headed toward Portsmouth. Instead, on the night of October 22, the fleet sailed into the dangerous waters of the Scilly Isles, about twenty miles west of the tip of England. The flagship, H.M.S. *Association*, struck rocks and sunk instantly. Three of the other four ships were also lost. In all, nearly two thousand English sailors died, including Admiral Shovell himself.

This incident was unusual for its time only in the number of lives lost. In the early eighteenth century, European sailors simply did not have the proper tools to navigate accurately and safely. Once their ships sailed out of sight of land, they could not tell where they were or exactly where they were going. In the Age of Exploration — the era beginning in the fifteenth century when such European sea captains as Christopher Columbus sailed the seven seas — every one of these explorers got lost at one time or another.

Opposite
In the Age of Exploration, navigators had no way to determine their exact position when storms blew a ship off course.

31

Beginning with Ptolemy in the second century A.D., geographers had worked with astronomers to map the known areas of the earth with lines of latitude and longitude. Latitude measures the distance south or north of the equator; it can be determined relatively easily, by calculations based on the position of the North Star. Longitude, which measures the distance east or west of a fixed point, is a different matter. The problem for sailors was that they had no reliable way to check their longitude once they were out of sight of land. Admiral Shovell's navigators knew how far north they were but had miscalculated how far west they were of Portsmouth.

To avoid getting lost, sailors hugged coastlines whenever possible. If they were sailing to European colonies in the Americas, they headed directly south until they reached the known latitude of their destination, then turned westward and tried to stay on a straight course across the Atlantic. But it was not always possible to hug the coastline (Admiral Shovell, for example, had every reason to steer clear of France) and doing so would make for a longer journey.

Until John Harrison presented his chronometric clock H-4 to the Royal Navy in 1760, the compass and the astrolabe were the best navigational tools available. Sir Francis Drake is reputed to have owned this 1569 composite "astronomical compendium," which included a compass and a tide table.

LAPIS POLARIS, MAGNES.

Lapis reclusit iste Flauio abditum   *Poli suum hunc amorem, at ipse nauitæ.*

Clocks and time were at the heart of the solution to the problem of determining longitude. It all comes down to mathematics. In geometry we learn that any circle — even the earth — can be divided into 360 equal wedges, or degrees. It takes the earth twenty-four hours to turn these 360 degrees, completing one cycle of day and night. Divide both figures by twenty-four, and we see that just as twenty-four hours is equivalent to 360 degrees, one hour is equivalent to 15 degrees. Therefore, if two places on the planet have exactly a one-hour time difference (that is, they reach high noon one hour apart), the distance between them is equivalent to 15 degrees of longitude.

In the sixteenth century, the Flemish astronomer Gemma Frisius theorized that two accurate clocks taken aboard a ship could be used to determine

In the sixteenth century, a roomful of navigational and astronomical instruments — and a lot of work on the part of an expert — added up to imprecise measurements.

33

longitude based on this mathematical equivalence. One clock would remain set to show the time in the home port. The second would be reset, according to the sun, at high noon each day. The difference between the two clocks could then be converted into degrees of longitude. For instance, if the home port clock read 2:00 P.M. at high noon on sea, that two hours of difference would signify two times 15, or 30 degrees of longitude. This would mean that the ship was 30 degrees west of its home port.

Unfortunately, in Frisius's time no clocks existed that were accurate enough to be used in this manner. It would be two hundred years before his theory could be put to the test.

For several years, the English navy agonized over how to prevent further tragedies like the loss of Admiral Shovell's fleet. In July 1714, Parliament passed the Longitude Act, which set a reward of £20,000 (the equivalent of almost $2 million today) for an accurate method of determining longitude. It established a Board of Longitude, which included the royal astronomer, to review the submis-

Dead reckoning enabled navigators to estimate a ship's speed and then make an educated guess about its position. Sailors tied a log to a very long rope in which knots had been made at regular intervals. When the log was heaved overboard, the ship's navigator let the rope run through his fingers and counted the knots as they went by. Meanwhile, a sailor measured the time that elapsed with a tiny sand-glass. The navigator used the number of knots he counted in that amount of time to figure out how fast the ship was traveling.

sions and supervise the necessary testing.

No one at the time suspected that the man who would finally solve the problem was a humble craftsman from a small village in the north of England. John Harrison was born in Yorkshire on March 24, 1693, the first child of a carpenter named Henry Harrison. A few years later, Henry Harrison moved his growing family (there were eventually five children) to Barrow, a town about sixty miles away in Lincolnshire.

John Harrison learned woodworking from his father. He played the viola and had other musical talents; eventually he would ring the Barrow church bells and serve as choirmaster. Unlike many children of people who worked with their hands in eighteenth-century England, Harrison learned to read and write. In fact, he had an eager interest in books. A clergyman visiting the Barrow church around 1712 gave him a book of Cambridge University science lectures, and the young man copied out the entire volume, annotating all the diagrams, and read the material very carefully over the next several years. He also studied Isaac Newton's *Principia*, in which the scientific genius presented the laws of gravity.

No one knows how John Harrison learned clockmaking, but in villages like Barrow, a carpenter had to be a master of all trades. There was no clockmaker of record working in the area then, so he must have taught himself, perhaps by taking clocks apart to study their movements or by repairing them.

In 1713 John Harrison built a pendulum clock. The twenty-year-old man must have been satisfied with his creation, since he signed and dated the dial. With his brother James, Harrison built two other pendulum clocks in the next four years. All three clocks show that he was an ingenious craftsman, with a

The movement of Harrison's first pendulum clock (1713) shows his fine craftsmanship and careful attention to detail. Harrison signed the dial, right above the Roman numerals VII through V.

JOHN HARRISON *born* 1693 *at* Foulby *near* Pontefract, YORKSHIRE;
Inventor *of the* Compound Pendulum *&c of several* Time Keepers, *for ascertaining the* LONGITUDE *at* Sea;
The last of which, on a Voyage, *ordered by the* Commissioners *of* Longitude, *was certified to have succeeded considerably within the Limits prescribed*
by the Act *of* Parliament, *of the* 12th *Year of* Queen Ann.

strong grasp of the technology needed to make a clock's movement run as accurately as was then possible. Harrison was unable to afford the brass that was then used in most clocks, so he made his clocks almost totally out of wood.

Around 1720 the Harrisons were commissioned to build a turret clock above a new stable at Brocklesby Park, the manor house of Sir Charles Pelham near Barrow. This time, Harrison used lignum vitae, an expensive tropical hardwood that exudes its own oil, so no further lubrication was necessary. Since the usual oils would clot or change in texture with changes in temperature (causing clocks to run too fast or too slow, or to stop running altogether), this was a step in the right direction. Harrison also invented the so-called grasshopper escapement, which not only ensured that all gears turned at the correct rate, but reduced friction as well as wear and tear. The turret clock was so well built that it is still running today.

By 1727, with considerable clockmaking experience under his belt, Harrison turned his sights to the longitude prize. He knew that even the best pendulum would malfunction while at sea, so he would have to find another way of powering the clock's movement. He wanted to build a clock that would run accurately on water, enabling it to determine longitude in the manner that Gemma Frisius had envisioned.

Harrison worked up plans for a new clock that was powered by a mainspring, not a pendulum. The energy released as the spring unwound would power a pair of balances, which moved like seesaws in opposite directions. He thought they would counterbalance each other, enabling the clock to be stable enough to run true even aboard a ship sailing through rough waters. In the summer of 1730, he traveled to London to show the plans to one member of the Board of Longitude, the famed astronomer Edmond Halley (who "discovered" Halley's Comet). Halley was impressed, but he knew that other board members would not look with an open mind at the ideas of a young, rural carpenter. So Halley suggested Harrison consult with George Graham, the foremost English clockmaker of the time. Although Harrison feared that Graham might

Opposite
John Harrison poses with two of his magnificent clocks. H-4 sits beside his right hand; behind him is H-3.

steal his ideas, he spent a day with the older man and won him over. Harrison later recalled, "The ice broke . . . and indeed he became at last vastly surprised at the thoughts or methods I had taken."

Graham gave Harrison an interest-free loan so he could build the clock he envisioned, and Harrison spent five years on this device, which has come to be called H-1. This marvelous creation, which incorporated the technological advances of Harrison's earlier clocks, is on display at the National Maritime Museum in Greenwich, England. It looks a bit like a ship. Four dials in front show the seconds, minutes, hours, and days. Two bar balances rise behind the dials like tall masts on a clipper ship. Linked to each other with wire and springs, they swing back and forth steadily as they count each second.

Around the time that H-1 was finished, Harrison moved his family — by now he and his wife, Elizabeth, had a son and a daughter — to London. He showed H-1 to George Graham and others, who were suitably impressed. Graham wrote, "John Harrison [has] with great labor and expense contrived

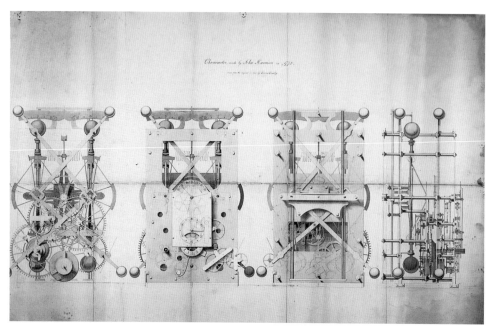

and executed a machine for measuring time at sea, upon such [principles] as seem to us to promise a very great and sufficient degree of exactness. We are of [the] opinion [that] it highly deserves public encouragement."

As a test in May 1736, Harrison and H-1 boarded H.M.S. *Centurion* to Lisbon. The trip was a rough one, and Harrison was terribly seasick. On this short, one-week crossing, the results were inconclusive. Harrison and his clock returned to England on H.M.S. *Orford*, and this journey, delayed by unfavorable winds and gales, proved a better test. As they neared the south coast of England after a month at sea, Captain Roger Wills assumed that the first land they sighted was Start Point, near Dartmouth. Making longitude calculations based on the time shown by H-1, Harrison countered that it was Lizard Point, some sixty miles to the west. He was right. A year later, Captain Wills wrote an affidavit recounting the incident and praising the accuracy of H-1.

On June 30, 1837, the Board of Longitude met to consider Harrison's clock. The eight commissioners, including Sir Edmond Halley, were kindly disposed toward H-1 as a result of the Lisbon trial, so when Harrison spoke about what he saw as "defects" in H-1 and asked for time to improve the mechanism and make a smaller clock, they agreed to finance his work. Harrison in turn promised that upon completion of a successful trial both clocks would become the government's property.

Three and a half years later, in January 1741, Harrison presented his new clock, H-2, to the Board of Longitude. H-2 turned out to be heavier and larger than its predecessor (eighty-six pounds as opposed to H-1's seventy-five pounds), but it did fit into a smaller box. The board had it tested and reported that H-2's motion was "sufficiently regular and exact for finding the longitude of a ship within the nearest limits proposed by Parliament and probably much nearer."

John Harrison ignored the praise and once more asked for money so that he could continue his work. Now forty-eight, he pressed on with his work with his son, William, as his partner. It would take him fifteen years to complete the next model, H-3, as he struggled with solving the problems of the effects of temperature change, friction, and irregularity.

During the many years Harrison was devising better machines, the Board of Longitude considered other proposals.

One of the wilder ones was the wounded dog theory. It used the "powder of sympathy," which (it was claimed) could heal wounds from a distance. If one applied the powder to an article of clothing or a bandage belonging to an injured person, the wound would heal, no matter how far away the person was. To apply this theory to the longitude problem, all one had to do was send a wounded dog aboard a ship. Someone would stay onshore and dip a bandage the dog had worn into the powder every day at noon. The theory was that the wounded dog would let out a yelp at the exact moment the powder

Royal Astronomer Edmond Halley was an enthusiastic supporter of Harrison's work.

was applied to its old bandage, which would tell the captain it was high noon at the home port.

The lunar-distance method, on the other hand, was a serious competitor for the longitude prize. This technique depended on observing the position of the moon against the stars and then making a series of calculations. Establishing a ship's position this way could take as much as four hours, and it required a clear night, flawless observations, an accurate clock, and the use of detailed tables to convert the readings into a precise longitude. It was easy for a mistake to be introduced at any point. Nevertheless, the lunar-distance method had many supporters. Scientists around Europe had worked on compiling the information in the tables, so, inevitably, they supported this approach. And some members of the Board of Longitude, especially the astronomers, still regarded Harrison as nothing more than a carpenter with no formal education who was wasting years — and the board's money — in pursuit of a dream.

By 1757, John and William Harrison were finally ready to present H-3 to the board. At sixty pounds, the lightest of the series thus far, H-3 featured a new way of compensating for temperature changes. Since steel and brass have different reactions to heat, Harrison riveted strips of the two metals together and used this bi-metallic strip in the clock's construction. The bi-metallic strip is still used today in thermostats and other temperature-sensitive devices. Although this smaller clock needed oil for lubrication, Harrison reduced friction by using finely cut jewels as bearings. Like his earlier timekeepers, H-3 has maintaining power, so it keeps running even as it is being wound; earlier clocks had stopped momentarily while being wound.

Even as he had put the finishing touches on H-3, John Harrison was already thinking about an entirely different approach. He wanted to make the clock much smaller. He told the board that he had "good reason to think" that a pocket watch could be "of great service with respect to the longitude."

Two years later, in 1759, he finished H-4, which at five inches in diameter and three pounds, fits neatly into an adult's hand. Considering the direction

Harrison had been working in for nearly thirty years, H-4 is an amazing reversal. He miniaturized parts where possible and came up with new solutions when miniaturization wasn't feasible. He jettisoned his grasshopper escapement in favor of a refined version of the verge escapement, an older variety. He used the bimetallic strip from H-3 to minimize the effect of temperature change on the mainspring.

John Harrison presented H-4 to the Board of Longitude in 1760, and it allowed him one more winter to fine-tune it before sending both H-3 and H-4 on a test run to the West Indies. This was the next step in the board's trial. Now in his late sixties, and no doubt recalling how seasick he was during H-1's trip to Lisbon, Harrison asked his son, William, to accompany his latest creation onboard. The following spring, William Harrison went to the port of Portsmouth, but waited five months for the order to sail. He suspected that supporters of the lunar-distance method on the board were holding up the trial while a young British astronomer, Nevil Maskelyne, was testing the rival method in the South Atlantic.

When the Harrisons finally got the go-ahead in November 1761, John Harrison withdrew H-3 from the trial. He was putting all his bets on the smaller H-4. With Captain Dudley Digges in command, H.M.S. *Deptford* sailed for Jamaica. H-4 was put under lock and key to prevent tampering, and William's daily winding of the watch was supervised.

After they were under way, Captain Digges discovered that a large portion

Harrison learned an enormous amount during the fifteen years it took him to build H-3. While the clock pleased the Board of Longitude, Harrison decided he wanted to take a different approach.

of the supplies — cheese and most of the beer, which was the main drink carried on board for sailors and passengers — had spoiled. He ordered them thrown overboard and set sail for the Portuguese island of Madeira, where *Deptford* could lay in more food and drink. The ship's log reads, "This day all the beer was expended; the people obliged to drink water."

Calculating the longitude from the time shown by H-4, William Harrison promised the concerned crew that they were within a day of the island. The ship's navigator thought they were one hundred miles farther away. The next morning, Madeira loomed into view, and soon the ship was restocked with fresh supplies. H-4 had won the confidence of the crew and the respect of the captain, who told William that he would buy one of the marine timekeepers as soon as John Harrison put them up for sale. Before hoisting anchor, Captain Digges wrote to the old clockmaker, advising him "of the great perfection of your watch in making the island."

When the ship finally landed in Port Royal, Jamaica, late on January 19, 1762, H-4 was found to be just 5.1 seconds slow.

Two days later, William Harrison and H-4 boarded H.M.S. *Merlin*, a tiny sloop-of-war, for the voyage back to England. It was a very rough crossing, and William worried about H-4's getting soaked by the high waves that often broke across the deck. Still, after landing in England on March 26, H-4 was accurate to within two minutes from the moment it had left England the previous November.

John Harrison had proved that a clock could tell a sailor exactly where on the high seas he was. He had presented the world with the first chronometric clock, or chronometer, as H-4 and succeeding generations of accurate and portable clocks designed to be used at sea came to be known. By rights, the Board of Longitude should have given him the full longitude prize then and there.

Unfortunately, the commissioners claimed that William had not followed the rules for the trial, and tension and conflict would pervade all dealings between the Harrisons and the board from then on.

In 1764 William Harrison took H-4 on another voyage for a further test, and though the Board of Longitude was "unanimously of [the] opinion that said timekeeper has kept its time within sufficient correctness," it paid the Harrisons only half the prize money. Then it demanded that they turn over H-4 and two copies of the clock before it would pay the other £10,000.

Infuriated, John Harrison eventually gave in. At the same time, the Board of Longitude asked another clockmaker, Larcum Kendall, to make a copy of the watch. Kendall's copy, which would come to be known as K-1, was finished first, in 1770. John Harrison completed H-5, his copy of H-4, in 1772.

Finally, in June 1773, thanks to the help of King George III, John Harrison received the money he was owed from Parliament, not from the Board of Longitude. In the long run, the board never awarded the longitude prize at all. Nevertheless, John Harrison had finally received his government's official recognition and thanks. He died three years later on his eighty-third birthday, March 24, 1776.

4
CLOCKS AND THE INDUSTRIAL REVOLUTION

The British were eager to capitalize on the potential of a precise portable marine timekeeper. The Royal Navy wanted to get one for each of its ships, but Harrison's chronometer was extremely expensive. Even K-1, the cheaper replica, cost about £450 (approximately $40,000 today).

The best clockmakers of the day studied Harrison's work. As they tried to create chronometers that were as accurate as Harrison's but that could be built quickly and less expensively, they devised simpler solutions to the problems of friction, irregularity, and temperature change. The key refinements came in the escapement. English clockmaker John Arnold tinkered with it to further reduce friction. His pocket chronometer No. 36 of 1779 was much smaller than H-4 and did not lose or gain more than three seconds a day in a thirteen-month trial. A few years later, his countryman Thomas Earnshaw invented an improved escapement that uses a lever (called a "detent") to regulate the beat. This device needed no oil on its teeth, which ensured its long, reliable performance. Earnshaw's escapement became the standard in chronometric clocks for the next 150 years.

Earnshaw could turn out a chronometer in about two months, partly because (like John Arnold) he farmed out the making of some parts, and his

Opposite
Large public clocks, like this one in Chester, England, were constructed during the Industrial Revolution to help factory workers get to work on time.

chronometers were priced low enough that the device was no longer a curiosity for the very wealthy. By the end of the 1780s, captains in the Royal Navy and of English merchant ships bound for India were buying chronometers from Earnshaw and others. Ten years later, at the turn of the century, the Royal Navy had its own supply of chronometers in Portsmouth. A navy captain sailing from that port could sign one out and take it to sea rather than buy his own. By 1815 there were about five thousand chronometers in circulation, the vast majority of which were British-made.

Because many British captains consulted chronometers, British ships generally reached their destinations more quickly and easily than the ships of other countries. As the expression "Britannia rules the waves" attests, Britain became the dominant naval power of the eighteenth and nineteenth centuries. It was during this period that Britain established its empire of colonies, so far-flung that another saying had it that "the sun never set on the British empire."

Without John Harrison's inventions and the productive clockmaking industry that followed in his footsteps, the reach of Britain's merchant marine would not have been so widespread, and its empire would not have expanded so quickly. And because England had the largest empire of any European country, more people grew up speaking English as their native or second language. These days, English has more than 340 million native speakers and is the language of international business, diplomacy, and trade.

There was one more important result of Britain's mastery of navigation. Sailors started using the position of Greenwich, England, as the prime meridian, or 0 degrees longitude, so that their calculations would correspond with each other. In 1884, an international conference made this common practice official, and today the prime meridian is paved right into the courtyard outside the old Royal Observatory buildings, just a few feet from the building where Harrison's clocks are on view. Visitors love to stand astride the meridian, with one foot planted in the Eastern Hemisphere and the other in the Western.

EARLY METHODS OF TELLING TIME

This early **sundial** indicated the time as the shadow of a horizontal stick fell across a specially marked board. Sundials cannot work on cloudy days or at night.

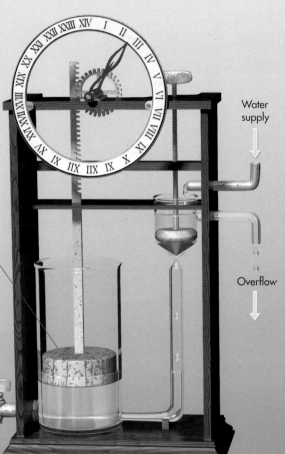

Water supply

Float

Overflow

This type of **water clock** was the first timekeeper to have a dial. Water entered a chamber from an overflowing supply tank through an adjustable valve. As the water filled the chamber, a float would rise on its surface, moving a mechanism to display the time on the dial. The chamber would have to be emptied daily to reset the dial.

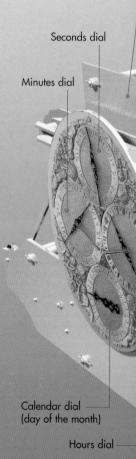

Main pla
frame of

Seconds dial

Minutes dial

Calendar dial
(day of the month)

Hours dial

The **candle clock** burned at a steady speed; marks indicated the time. A glass tube protected the candle from drafts that would increase the rate of burning.

The **sandglass** measured a specific interval of time. It would take a certain number of minutes for sand to pass from the upper chamber to the lower chamber.

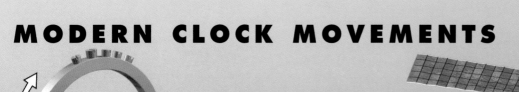

MODERN CLOCK MOVEMENTS

Electromechanical
The balance wheel is powered by a reversing electromagnetic field. Power for the electromagnet comes from a battery, eliminating the need to wind the mainspring daily.

Electronic Tuning Fork
The oscillations of an electromagnetically induced vibrating tuning fork measure out time. This watch is especially accurate since the timekeeping component is frictionless.

Atomic Vibration
The atomic clock uses the vibrations of cesium atoms to measure time and is so accurate that it is the benchmark by which time is set worldwide. Its time signals are broadcast via satellite and can be picked up by special watches.

Quartz Crystal
A weak electrical current causes the quartz crystal to vibrate. These regular vibrations control the clock's movement. Quartz watches are compact and use very little power.

BASIC PARTS OF THE WRISTWATCH

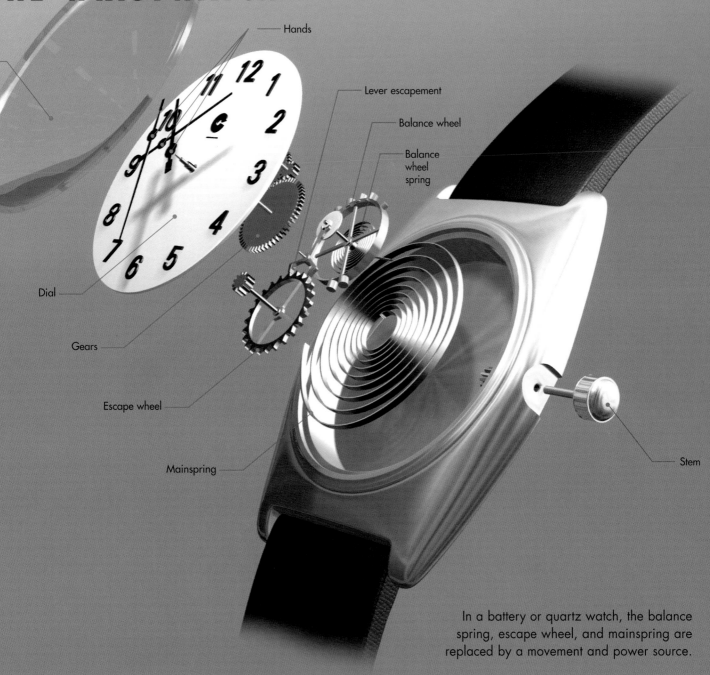

Hands

Lever escapement

Balance wheel

Balance wheel spring

Dial

Gears

Escape wheel

Mainspring

Stem

In a battery or quartz watch, the balance spring, escape wheel, and mainspring are replaced by a movement and power source.

THE ESCAPEMENT

The escapement takes the energy from the power source (for instance, a pendulum or a mainspring), transmits it through the gears, and releases it in "beats" (often, one per second) so that the clock or watch continuously shows the correct time.

The verge escapement relies upon the regular swing of a **pendulum**, permitting the wound-up clock mechanism to move forward at regularly timed increments.

At any given time, at least one of the two **verge pallets** is engaged with a tooth of the **crown wheel**, which is geared to the clock mechanism.

As the pendulum swings right, the rear verge pallet slips off the crown wheel tooth with which it is engaged. This allows the crown wheel to rotate slightly, until another tooth stops against the front verge pallet.

The pendulum then reverses direction. As it passes through the bottom of its swing, the rear verge pallet slips into position between — but does not touch — the next two teeth on the crown wheel.

As the pendulum swings left, the front verge pallet slips off the crown wheel tooth, and the crown wheel rotates further until its tooth stops against the rear verge pallet.

With each swing, the crown wheel is allowed to rotate by just one tooth. This means that the clock mechanism moves at a rate controlled by the regular swing of the pendulum.

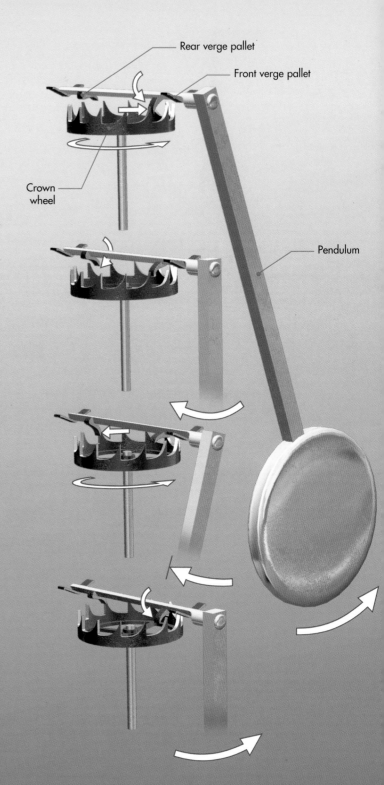

Rear verge pallet

Front verge pallet

Pendulum

Crown wheel

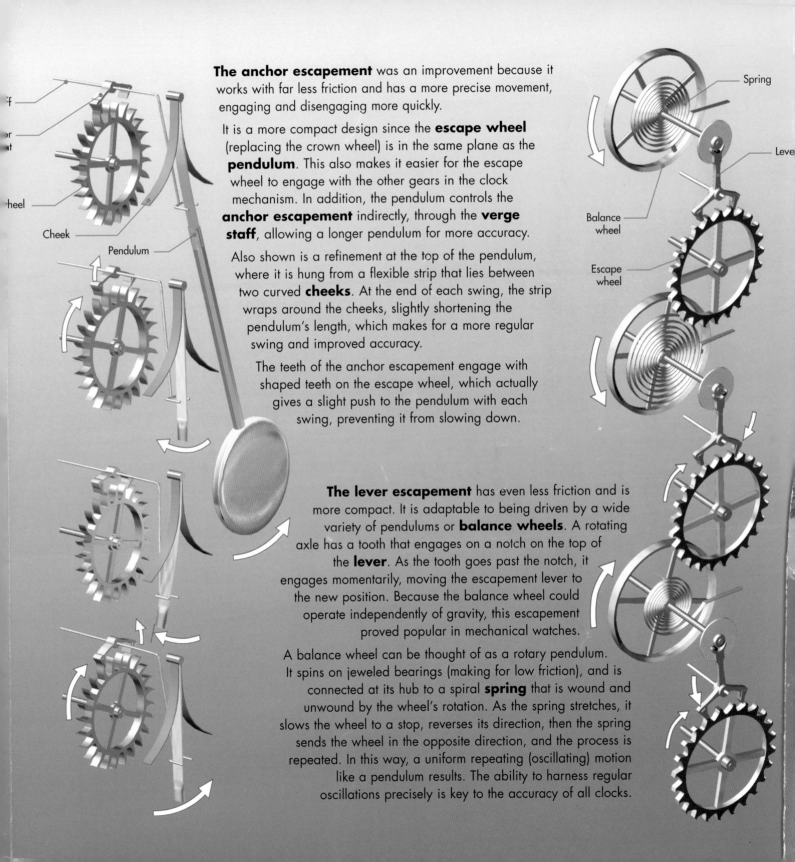

The anchor escapement was an improvement because it works with far less friction and has a more precise movement, engaging and disengaging more quickly.

It is a more compact design since the **escape wheel** (replacing the crown wheel) is in the same plane as the **pendulum**. This also makes it easier for the escape wheel to engage with the other gears in the clock mechanism. In addition, the pendulum controls the **anchor escapement** indirectly, through the **verge staff**, allowing a longer pendulum for more accuracy.

Also shown is a refinement at the top of the pendulum, where it is hung from a flexible strip that lies between two curved **cheeks**. At the end of each swing, the strip wraps around the cheeks, slightly shortening the pendulum's length, which makes for a more regular swing and improved accuracy.

The teeth of the anchor escapement engage with shaped teeth on the escape wheel, which actually gives a slight push to the pendulum with each swing, preventing it from slowing down.

The lever escapement has even less friction and is more compact. It is adaptable to being driven by a wide variety of pendulums or **balance wheels**. A rotating axle has a tooth that engages on a notch on the top of the **lever**. As the tooth goes past the notch, it engages momentarily, moving the escapement lever to the new position. Because the balance wheel could operate independently of gravity, this escapement proved popular in mechanical watches.

A balance wheel can be thought of as a rotary pendulum. It spins on jeweled bearings (making for low friction), and is connected at its hub to a spiral **spring** that is wound and unwound by the wheel's rotation. As the spring stretches, it slows the wheel to a stop, reverses its direction, then the spring sends the wheel in the opposite direction, and the process is repeated. In this way, a uniform repeating (oscillating) motion like a pendulum results. The ability to harness regular oscillations precisely is key to the accuracy of all clocks.

Cheek

Pendulum

Spring

Balance wheel

Escape wheel

Lever

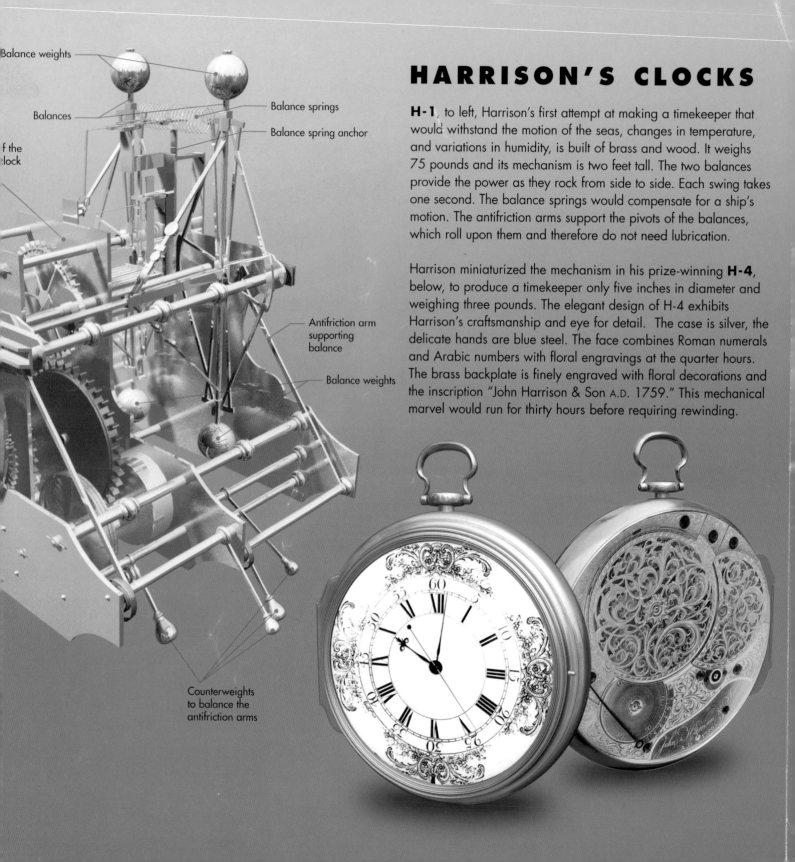

Balance weights

Balances

f the
lock

Balance springs

Balance spring anchor

Antifriction arm
supporting
balance

Balance weights

Counterweights
to balance the
antifriction arms

HARRISON'S CLOCKS

H-1, to left, Harrison's first attempt at making a timekeeper that would withstand the motion of the seas, changes in temperature, and variations in humidity, is built of brass and wood. It weighs 75 pounds and its mechanism is two feet tall. The two balances provide the power as they rock from side to side. Each swing takes one second. The balance springs would compensate for a ship's motion. The antifriction arms support the pivots of the balances, which roll upon them and therefore do not need lubrication.

Harrison miniaturized the mechanism in his prize-winning **H-4**, below, to produce a timekeeper only five inches in diameter and weighing three pounds. The elegant design of H-4 exhibits Harrison's craftsmanship and eye for detail. The case is silver, the delicate hands are blue steel. The face combines Roman numerals and Arabic numbers with floral engravings at the quarter hours. The brass backplate is finely engraved with floral decorations and the inscription "John Harrison & Son A.D. 1759." This mechanical marvel would run for thirty hours before requiring rewinding.

While Harrison and others were struggling to improve the chronometer, stationary timekeepers — longcase clocks, table clocks, and large public clocks — had become accurate to within seconds. It now made much more sense than it ever had before for all kinds of people to pay attention to the time.

Starting around 1750, the Industrial Revolution, a century of massive technological innovation and unprecedented change, produced enormous transformations in the way people worked, in how and where they lived, and in the ways in which goods were made and sold. Many important inventions played a role in this transformation. Chief among them were the steam engine and the new generation of highly accurate clocks.

Everyone's lives were affected by industrialization, but working people saw their daily existence change the most of all. They swarmed into rapidly expand-

London's Big Ben is perhaps the most famous public clock in the world. The clock tower rises 316 feet high, dwarfing the Houses of Parliament. Big Ben's enormous dial is twenty-three feet wide.

ing towns and cities, trading the life of a farm laborer for that of a factory worker. They left behind their families and a close-knit rural community hoping that higher wages would make up for the cramped, miserable quarters in the slums. In factories they were trained to operate machinery designed to forge one individual part, drill a hole through it, or rivet it to another part. Once they had mastered such a very specific task, they were assigned to do it all day. (This is called specialization of labor.)

Workers had to adjust to not doing their jobs independently. Much of the production process in factories had to be performed in a certain order. One worker had to finish task A before the next could begin task B. Therefore, it was

A clock-keeper winds Big Ben's mechanism in 1959.

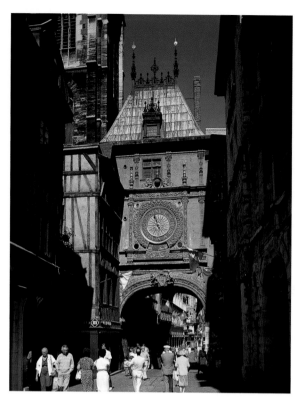

extremely important for them all to follow the same schedule. First, they had to arrive at a set hour. This involved getting up early enough and allowing enough time to get to the workplace (although there were horse-driven streetcars, most people walked to work). Some factories sent "wakers" (also called "knockers up") to their employees' homes. These men would knock on a door or rap on a window, acting as human alarm clocks.

Once workers arrived at the plant, the day was structured according to a strict plan. The sequence of events was announced by a series of time cues, often loud whistles. One sounded at the beginning of a shift, others at the start and finish of each break or mealtime, and the last at the end of a shift. Clocks also regulated factory workers' income: They were often paid by the hour, replacing the per-piece wage system of earlier, small-scale manufacturing and

the fixed rate received by most agricultural workers. Soon, very good workers began to be rewarded with clocks or watches (the better to be punctual), and those who were chronically late were docked wages based on how many minutes of the workday they had missed.

Factory buildings were constructed with large clocks to announce the time to all, and everyone grew to rely on these prominent clocks as well as those in church towers or on municipal buildings. All activities related to trade and manufacturing — from the delivery of raw materials to the distribution of finished goods, from appointments with salespeople to the hours that a store was open — demanded that people pay attention to what time it was.

Clockmaking itself benefited from improvements in manufacturing. Although earlier clockmakers had used lathes occasionally to craft pendulum rods, a

Left
Especially if they're running late, travelers at this Paris train station are better off checking the clock in the background than this eye-catching sculpture.

Right
Harold Lloyd's famous stunt in the film *Safety Last* (1923) made memorable use of a public clock.

Longcase clocks remained in vogue for hundreds of years; this beautiful model from Chippendale dates from 1790. Henry Clay Work's song "Grandfather's Clock" (1875) was so popular that it inspired the name by which we commonly know these clocks today.

GRANDFATHER'S CLOCK

WRITTEN AND COMPOSED   SUNG WITH GREAT SUCCESS
H. C. WORK.   J. B. FERRELL.
Of the MOHAWK MINSTRELS
(AGRICULTURAL HALL LONDON)
ALSO SUNG BY
JOHN READ AND CHAS CLIFFORD.
LONDON.

skilled craftsperson usually made all the parts for a clock by hand. This was a laborious process, and no two parts were identical from clock to clock. Then, in the eighteenth and nineteenth centuries, machines were developed to make gears. Using these mass-produced gears, clocks became easier to build and cheaper to sell. Once the price of clocks decreased, they became a common feature in more and more homes, where shelf clocks were the most popular model, and prosperous wage earners carried pocket watches, usually in their vest pockets.

Although clockmaking benefited from the growth of manufacturing in Europe, the change from a craft to an industry took place in America, most prominently in New England.

In 1807 Eli Terry, a Connecticut clockmaker, contracted with two merchants to produce four thousand clocks with wooden gears in three years; at this time, few clockmakers produced more than twenty clocks annually, and none made more than two hundred a year. Terry knew he could never make his deadline in the conventional way, with each clockmaker making one clock, from start to finish, at a time. He designed a new type of timekeeper made of individual components that could be manufactured separately. No matter who made each part, it was standardized, or interchangeable, and would fit into the others in the same way. Terry spent an enormous amount of time planning how to mass-produce the clocks and adapting his machinery to the water power provided

Eli Terry's Connecticut clockmaking factory turned out inexpensive and attractive shelf clocks like this in the early 1800s. Terry brought mass-production techniques to the clockmaking industry and affordable clocks to almost everyone.

by Connecticut's rivers. Because of this, no clocks were finished in the first year, but Terry made about a thousand clocks in his second year, and the next year he produced three times as many.

Terry's ability to fulfill this large order ushered in a new era of clock manufacturing. By applying the processes of mass production, he could make timekeepers so inexpensively that the price of his clocks plummeted. For the first time in history, the working class could afford to buy clocks. The devices were peddled in all frontiers of the young country. Terry's wooden clock was replaced in the 1840s by an inexpensive clock with a brass movement that was introduced in 1839 by Chauncey Jerome. By 1855 more than half a million inexpensive clocks were being manufactured annually in Connecticut.

These brass clocks and, after 1857, machine-made American watches were sold in great numbers domestically and exported to Europe and else-

where. Many European clock- and watchmakers of the latter half of the nineteenth century resisted adopting mass-production techniques and were content to supply limited quantities of finely made timekeepers to the wealthy few.

The coming of the railroad was another key step in the rapid industrialization and urbanization taking place in western Europe and North America. As railroads linked one town to the next, people and goods could move from place to place more quickly and easily than ever before.

For centuries, each town had set its clocks against the sun, using high noon as the calibration point. This meant that the time in two towns fifty miles apart, east to west, was slightly different. The small discrepancy was not a large problem when towns were linked by slow-moving stagecoaches, and when trade and movement between neighboring counties was limited. But it became a serious

PHINEAS PINCHBECK
SELLS
DOLLY-VARDEN ALARM-CLOCKS

APPRENTICES' TIMEKEEPERS
FOR MANUFACTURERS

hurdle once an extensive network of railway lines was built.

Trains ran according to a printed schedule. But whose time was to be used, when each station's local time varied by seconds or even minutes? Crews and passengers were confused, and going by the "wrong" time could mean passengers were left behind; worse, there were serious head-on collisions because of mix-ups over timetables.

In Britain in the mid-nineteenth century, the various independent railway companies instituted "railway time" to fix this mess. Each railway line decreed that the time in its terminus, or in a large city such as London, would be the official time for that whole line. Using another new invention, the telegraph, the railroad could set railway time at the central office and send it almost instantly to all the local stations. For the next decade or so, every train station in Britain displayed two different times, the local time and the railway time, and passengers were instructed to follow the latter.

Still, this system had its flaws, so in 1847, the railway companies got together and decreed that all railroad timetables in the country would be based on the time in Greenwich. The British Post Office endorsed the plan and com-

Above
In the late nineteenth and early twentieth centuries, American clocks were made in an astonishing variety of designs.

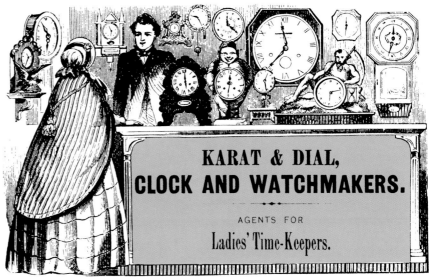

municated precise time signals over telegraph wires, so that every city, town, and village nationwide was finally operating according to the same time.

This worked well in a country the size of Great Britain, but it would not suffice in the large nations of North America. It would be impractical for the time in Washington, D.C. — or anywhere else — to be used across the entire United States. It was not until the 1880s that a solution was devised: time zones, broad areas that would keep the same time, one hour later than the time zone to the east.

In 1884, an international conference agreed to divide the earth up into twenty-four time zones. The official British time, now called Greenwich Mean Time, would serve as the base from which time in other parts of the world would be calculated. Finally, the entire planet was brought under one system of telling time. That the time-zone system was based on the time in Greenwich, the official site of 0 degrees longitude and the home of John Harrison's revolutionary eighteenth-century clocks, seems like a well-deserved tribute to the genius of English clockmakers.

The Waterbury (Connecticut) Clock Company made this pendulum to fit into a variety of models.

Right
By the late nineteenth century, pocket watches, such as this 1890 model made by the Rockford Watch Company, were being used by almost everyone.

Below right
Always late for a very important date, the White Rabbit in Lewis Carroll's *Alice's Adventures in Wonderland* (1865) checks his pocket watch in this classic illustration by Sir John Tenniel.

Far right
A conductor consults his pocket watch and signals the train's engineer. Precise timekeeping is vital to the smooth operation of a railroad.

Opposite
The prime meridian runs through the National Maritime Museum in Greenwich, England, former site of the Royal Observatory.

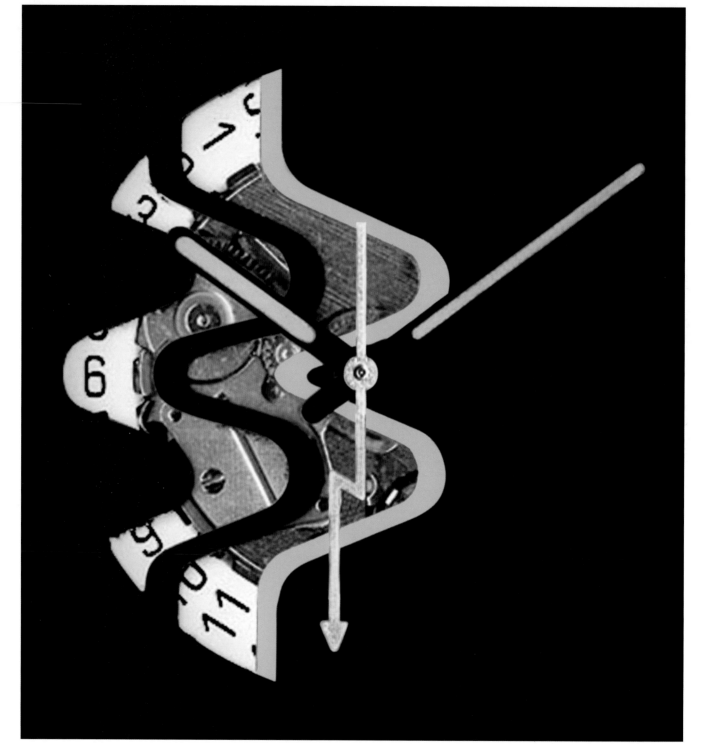

5

THE FUTURE OF TIME

In its first centuries, as it developed from a sundial to a factory-produced system of gears and gadgets, the clock couldn't have evolved much more dramatically. But the last 150 years have hardly been less extraordinary. If anything, the pace of change and progress in clockmaking increased in the twentieth century.

Today's new materials, including the alloys invar and elinvar (for use in clocks and watches, respectively), are better able than John Harrison's bimetallic strip to reduce the effect of temperature change on timekeepers. And new manufacturing tools and techniques have continued to drive prices down and make clocks more accurate and more affordable.

There have also been tremendous breakthroughs in how to power the clock. In the mid-nineteenth century, Alexander Bain, a Scot working in London, experimented with electricity in clocks. He proved that a steady electrical current could power a motor, which would move a clock's gears, and by 1852 a battery-powered electric clock was installed at the Royal Observatory in Greenwich. But Bain was ahead of his time: Electric clocks would not be practical until offices, homes, and factories had been wired to receive electricity from a power plant — a development still more than a generation away. (The

Opposite
The end of the twentieth century brought watch designs that would have been unthinkable only a few years earlier.

first commercial generating station in the United States opened in New York City in 1882.)

From the 1930s on, as pocket watches began to give way to more convenient wristwatches, inventors became interested in making them easier to wind. Like older clocks, wristwatches had to be wound regularly, or the devices would stop telling time. For centuries a key was used to do the job with shelf clocks, longcase clocks, and many pocket watches, but a tiny winding wheel, called a stem, on the edge of the watch was now developed.

After World War II, clockmakers turned their attention to using miniature batteries. The Hamilton Watch Company worked on prototypes for more than a decade, since it wanted a battery-powered watch to keep time as accurately as conventional models did and demanded that the battery last for at least a year. These watches — confusingly called electric watches — were introduced in 1957 and dominated the market within a few years.

Early in the twentieth century, the French scientist Pierre Curie had discovered that quartz crystals vibrate at a fixed rate when electricity is passed through them. By 1929 a Canadian named W. A. Marrison had used the energy from this vibration to power a clock, but such timekeepers did not become widespread until the early 1970s. These days, energy from a tiny battery inside the timekeeper makes the piece of quartz crystal vibrate, and a microchip converts the vibration into a signal that powers the gears that turn the clock's hands to show the time. Because the entire process is electronic, not mechanical, it is not affected by changes in temperature or air pressure. Quartz crystals have become the standard. They are used in most wristwatches and many clocks today.

Quartz watches and clocks now use synthetic crystals, most of which come from Japan, which has replaced Switzerland as the center of the world's clock-making industry. Any quartz watch or clock, even an inexpensive brand, is more accurate than the finest precision clocks available a century ago. It will gain or lose no more than one minute a year.

Quartz watches are only one kind of timekeeper we see these days with digital displays. Not only are these displays often easier to read — you don't need to know how to tell time to read them — but they have dramatically changed how people answer the age-old question, "What time is it?" It used to be customary to round off the time to the nearest five-minute interval. But with a digital watch, we report the time to the exact minute, just as it is shown on the display: "It's 2:22."

In fact, an increased emphasis on accuracy and precision in all aspects of life has marked the twentieth century. All the different clocks we refer to in our lives — electric wall clocks and clock radios, clocks built into microwave ovens and videocassette recorders, quartz wristwatches, and others — provide time as accurately as we need in everyday life.

Nevertheless, extremely specialized tasks require exceptionally precise timekeeping. In automated manufacturing processes, actions must be timed to tiny increments of a second, and an error of even a small fraction of a second can have serious effects on the durability or performance of a part. Even tiny inaccuracies in timekeeping could have dire effects on scientific research, especially astronomy and space travel. Such precision is also required by advanced medical equipment, such as magnetic resonance imaging (MRI) machines, which take pictures of the inside of the body.

Today's standard is set by the atomic clock, which grew out of scientific studies of the properties of the atom in the middle of the twentieth century. Physicists who noticed that an atom seemed to vibrate at a regular rate

Opposite
An early electric clock (about 1845) made by Alexander Bain. The electricity was provided by an enormous battery. Electric clocks would remain curiosities and the object of scientific research for more than a generation, until cities began to be wired for electricity.

theorized that the atom could be harnessed to help determine the time, and in 1955 a joint team of American and British scientists used the atoms of the element cesium to complete the world's first atomic clock.

This and later atomic clocks keep time at an almost unimaginable level of accuracy; they lose or gain only one second every three thousand years. The United States and Great Britain adapted atomic time as their official government time in 1958. By 1972, when a standard called Universal Time (UTC) was adopted, most of the world had followed suit. Under UTC, time is defined atomically, not astronomically. Earlier, a second was a tiny subdivision of a system based on observations of the earth's revolution on its own axis and its journey around the sun. Under UTC a second is the time it takes an atom of a certain kind of cesium to vibrate 9,192,631,770 times.

Atomic clocks have proven that the earth itself is not a perfect timekeeper. Through the kinds of close observation that are now possible, scientists have determined that our planet's revolution around the sun sometimes varies. As a result, there are tiny differences between atomic time and the earth's time. To compensate for these, "leap seconds" are now periodically inserted into atomic time. The most recent leap second was inserted at 7:00 P.M., Eastern Standard Time, on December 31, 1998.

Starting with the alarm clock and the clock radio, the clock's role has steadily expanded. All cooking in microwave ovens is precisely measured by a built-in

Right
The first battery-powered wristwatch was the "electric watch" produced by the Hamilton Watch Company in the late 1950s. Miniature batteries, developed for use in World War II, were quickly adapted to other uses in peacetime.

timekeeper, for example, and we can program videocassette recorders to tape a program because of the clock that is part of the mechanism. But it's the computer that has put the clock to the widest range of other uses. Computer networks in schools and offices could not function without being regulated by interior timekeepers. These built-in clocks control such functions as directing individual computers of the network to periodically save work and scheduling system maintenance for hours when most of the employees are not at their desks. A personal computer has a built-in timer, too, which among other things enables it to send E-mail hours after it's written.

The future of the clock lies in the same direction, in its association with new machinery. Among the most promising innovations are so-called smart houses. Architects are already designing these technologically advanced homes, in which many of the features, such as heating and cooling, security, plumbing, and even cooking, will be controlled by a very powerful computer. That

Left
This quartz crystal watch with a digital display was made by the American manufacturer Waltham Watch Company around 1976.

Center
In a drive to promote this quartz watch as being more accurate and reliable than its competition in 1974, Seiko promoted it as "the watch that science built."

Right
The Junghans radio-controlled clock contains a mini-computer. It can pick up radio signals broadcast from the official U.S. atomic clock, so that it always keeps the precise time.

computer will perform its tasks according to how the clock inside it is set.

The computer's role as the key machine of the twenty-first century may even result in a fundamental change in the way we tell time. More and more business is conducted on the Internet, involving people in many different parts of the globe, each possibly in a different time zone. To simplify online timekeeping, Internet time has been proposed. In Internet time the day is divided into one thousand units of 1 minute 26.4 seconds each. A day in Internet time begins at midnight in Switzerland (home of the Swatch company, its inventor and proponent). The entire world would use the same time system, with @625, for example, being midafternoon in Switzerland and the start of the workday in Chicago. A wristwatch could display local time and Internet time.

Some high-tech capabilities will also be incorporated into the wristwatch.

In 1933 the Ingersoll-Waterbury Company introduced the first Mickey Mouse watch. The model's success rescued the company from bankruptcy during the Depression.

Beginning in 1983, Swatch made the wristwatch a versatile and fun fashion accessory as well as an affordable timepiece. More than 2,300 different designs have been created through 1999. Swatch's Net-Time Beat model (*above*) displays Internet time and local time.

A GPS watch — one that gets information from the global positioning system, a series of satellites constantly orbiting the earth — was introduced in 1999. The watch can give you not only the time but also your precise latitude and longitude.

Even if your wristwatch won't be able to tell you where you are, it undoubtedly will include many functions other than telling time, such as acting as a telephone or pager, displaying written messages, monitoring air quality, or letting you know which homework assignment is due when. Accuracy will be a given. In fact, there's already a watch today that is able to reset itself by contacting the official atomic clock via a radio signal bounced off a satellite.

Of course, watches will also continue to be fashion accessories, since these days it's not just collectors who have a lot of them. Some people love to wear a colorful Swatch one day, a Mickey Mouse watch the next, and a traditional leather-banded wristwatch the day after that.

Future refinements in timekeeping will help humans explore the farther reaches of the solar system and beyond, because precise timing is vital to space travel. Satellites and spacecraft hurtling through the darkness of zero-gravity space for a rendezvous with a space station or a distant planet need to have carefully calculated courses. In fact, accurate timekeeping is as important to safe navigation in space as marine chronometers were to the ships that sailed the high seas in the 1700s and 1800s.

Measuring and calculating time is so basic to us now that we take it for granted, rarely stopping to think how difficult it would be if we had to run our lives with nothing more precise than a sundial. How the clocks built into the next generation of computers and electronic appliances will affect us remains to be seen. Meanwhile, the rhythm of life will continue to be ordained by the earth's progress around the sun, as it has for thousands of years, and people will organize their days based on the units of time that were gradually developed over the course of human history, referring to the timekeepers that great inventors such as John Harrison struggled so long to perfect.

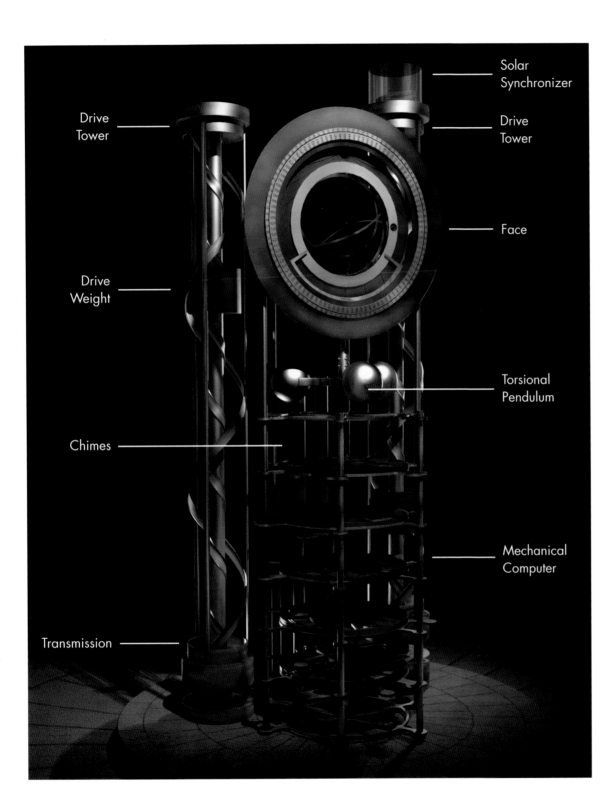

Solar
Synchronizer

Drive
Tower

Drive
Tower

Face

Drive
Weight

Torsional
Pendulum

Chimes

Mechanical
Computer

Transmission

The Clock of the Long
Now was designed by
computer scientist Danny
Hillis to last for the next
ten thousand years. His
eight-foot-tall prototype
is as much monument as
timekeeper, with much of
the movement visible
through glass. The clock
will tick once a year and
have a century hand that
will advance only once
every hundred years. A
cuckoo will emerge to
announce each new
millennium.

FURTHER READING

Betts, Jonathan. *Harrison.* London: National Maritime Museum, 1997.

Branley, Franlyn Mansfield. *Keeping Time: From the Beginning and into the 21st Century.* Boston: Houghton Mifflin, 1993.

Bruton, Eric. *The History of Clocks and Watches.* New York: Crescent/Crown, 1989.

Crosby, Alfred W. *The Measure of Reality: Quantification and Western Society, 1250-1600.* New York: Cambridge University Press, 1997.

Dale, Rodney. *Timekeeping.* New York: Oxford University Press, 1992.

Jespersen, James, and Jane Fitz-Randolph. *Time and Clocks for the Space Age.* New York: Atheneum, 1979.

Landes, David S. *Revolution in Time: Clocks and the Making of the Modern World.* Cambridge, Massachusetts: Belknap/Harvard University Press, 1983.

Sobel, Dava, and William J. H. Andrews, *The Illustrated Longitude: The True Story of a Lone Genius Who Solved the Greatest Scientific Problem of His Time.* New York: Walker, 1998.

INDEX

Produced by
CommonPlace Publishing
2 Morse Court
New Canaan, Connecticut 06840

The text and display for this book have been typeset in various weights and sizes of Futura. A sans serif face designed in Germany in 1928 by Paul Renner, Futura has been widely copied and adapted for digital type systems. Based upon geometric shapes, the Futura letter is characterized by lines of uniform width. Previous typefaces reflected the irregularities of hand lettering.

We wish to express our gratitude to Chris Bailey at the American Clock and Watch Museum in Bristol, Connecticut, to Jonathan Betts at the National Maritime Museum in Greenwich, England, and to Michael Friedman at the National Watch and Clock Museum in Columbia, Pennsylvania, whose advice and research enriched this book. Thanks also go to Paul De Angelis, Mitchell Bloom, Jeanne Palmer, Ilene Chazanof, David Heaps, Dorothy Crouch, and Dan Archambault for their help and support during the writing of this book. The index was prepared by Judith Kip.